Zack, you're right. In the end, it's the little things.

Posted February 16, 2014

Like & Share

Poems, Stories, and Statuses
By Joaquín Zihuatanejo

CoolSpeak Publishing Company

Book design by Joaquín Zihuatanejo, Carlos Ojeda Jr. and Coolspeak
Publishing Company.

Cover design by Carlos Ojeda Jr.

ISBN-13: **978-0692235423**

Also by Joaquín Zihuatanejo

Books

Family Tree

of fire and rain
a collaboration with natasha
carrizosa

Barrio Songs

Fight or Flight
forthcoming

Audio CDs

Barrio Songs

Stand Up and Be Heard

Live at Longwood

of fire and rain
a spoken word collaboration
with natasha carrizosa

Child of the Hood Days

HOPE 5 MILES

Barbaric Yawps
Best of Joaquín Zihuatanejo
for Students

Family Tree

Canciones del Barrio
Poemas en la Lengua de mi
Abuelo *forthcoming*

Order all Joaquín Zihuatanejo books and CDs at
www.jzthepoet.com

Order the EBook version of Like and Share,
Family Tree, Barrio Songs, and OF FIRE AND
RAIN at Online bookstores everywhere.

Contents

There is a scene in Superman, when Lois is in Superman's arms high above the city below, and they stare into each other's eyes as that beautiful music by John Williams is playing in the background, and then out of nowhere a voice over of Margot Kidder reading the worst poem in the history of poems happens. You know, the one with the lines, "Can you read my mind? Do you know what I'm thinking?" Aida, you and I are the only two people on this planet that I know of who are entirely shaken by the placement of such a bad poem in such a good movie. That entire scene is out of place. It's beautiful and ugly, it's graceful and awkward, all at the same time. Life is like that. So are we.

This book is for you. I hope it makes you smile.

After the Show

"Don't you dare go home until your last fan goes home."

—Loretta Lynn

I will sign your journal
Your book
My book
The phone book
I will answer any question
You have
For me
I will
Give advice to the young poet
Playwright
Actor
Teacher
I will laugh with you
I will cry with you
I will sign your backpack
Your forearm
Your forehead
I will sign treaties with you
I will sign on the dotted line
I will co-sign that loan with you
I will make
John Hancock jealous
By the sheer size of my signature
I will elaborate under it
With a phrase written in print
Something like
Award–winning teacher
Or World Champion Poet
Or Break Dance Enthusiast
So that many years from now
You will know
That this incoherent swirl of
Cursive is my signature
Yes, I will read you one more poem
Yes, I will take a photo with you
Yes, you can Facebook me
Yes, I do have a Twitter feed
You can follow me at...
Once after a one hour

Reading at a university
I stayed and talked
With a small group of students
For three hours
They invited me to go out for pizza after
And though I was tired
I went gladly
Because the only thing a poet loves more
Than the sound of his own voice
Is pizza

Posted April 7, 2012, subsequently removed for editing

Another Kind of Faith

1.

Somehow they
Heard about us
We, an inner city team
From the Lower East Side
That could not be beaten
They, a premier league team
From some far-off foreign suburb
That could not be beaten
The game was inevitable
It was Manifest Destiny
It was the Great Western Movement
It was the Alamo
It was the Mexican American War

2.

Were they any more American than we?
Their name,
The Cowboys,
Ours,
Aztecas
You cannot write this
Sometimes it simply is

3.

It is simple
Good guys wear white
Bad guys wear black
We were flashes of black during the warm ups
They nervously sized us up

4.

Days earlier, they invited us to their facility
That's what they called it, "facility"
In the barrio
We played on a field
That was two-thirds dirt
One-third dream

5.

The night before the game I dreamed of war
We were armed with staffs
Spears, bows and arrows
They with muskets and swords
I watched my friend die beside me.

6.

A "friendly"
That's the word they used
But there wasn't anything friendly about it

7.

Jesús Santos, my best friend
Jesús Santos, our best player
Jesús Santos, I watched you die in my dream
Jesús Santos, you sacrificed yourself for me
Jesús Santos, how many days before you rise
And save us

8.

Save us from their onslaught
Save us from our rage

9.

Some of us played with rage in our hearts,
But not Jesús
Only someone pure of heart
Could curve a ball like him
He was our leader
He was our savior
And we his ten disciples

10.

Ten minutes into the game
Jesús scored the first goal
They answered not long after
On a two on one breakaway.

11.

They wanted to break us because we were different
We wanted to break them because they were beautiful

12.

Jesús was a thing of beauty
Watching him weave through defenders
His eye never on the ball
Always ahead
It was part of him
He slept with a soccer ball
Kicked one to school and back home again
Left it outside the church
On Sunday morning
Resting on the steps
Waiting for him
Like a loyal pet
A small practice goal in his back yard
100 shots on goal every day of his youth
A different position
A different placement
A different scenario in his mind each time

13.

100 shots X 365 days = another kind of faith

14.

This was another kind of cruelty
This was brutal
This was less slide
And more tackle
This was five on one
This was Cowboys vs. Indian
This was the wounded knee
Of the most beautiful soccer player to have ever lived
This was hit and run
This was freight train
Made of legs and arms and fists and cleats
This was Jesús Santos
Laid out on the field
Arms outstretched

Wailing in agony
This was crucifixion

Somehow they had turned us into beasts, made us more Mexican and less American that day. The fight that ensued was viscous, boys were not meant to fight like that, but sometimes war cannot be avoided, sometimes war is there waiting for you all along, sometimes it simply is. It is a simple thing to hate the way we did that day. Days earlier I had dreamt of war, watched my friend die beside me. Jesús Santos are you still out there, will you save us from the rage in our hearts? If we take a deep breath, if we count to ten, can we be young and innocent again? Did your heart break that day? Jesús please tell me, does one have to be just different or beautiful, or is it possible that one can be both? Jesús, we were once small things made of flesh and beauty and faith. That was so long ago, we've all been brutalized, wounded, broken since then, but I ask you, please, Jesús, tell me, is there any chance of resurrection?

A rough version of part 14 posted April 2012, subsequently removed for editing

The Naming Ceremony

My mother told me once
That my father and grandfather
Battled over my naming ceremony
Which is likely a lie
But a beautiful one nonetheless
So I choose not to protest
My grandfather wanted to name me Joaquín or Miguel
My father wanted to name me Royce or Dale
So I have one of each
My first name is browner
Than my grandfather's eyes
My middle name is whiter
Than my father's lies
I spy with my little eye
Something brown and white
When asked "What is your name?"
I only reply one thing
"My name is Joaquín."
But I actually have two names
Does that omission make me a liar
A half-breed archetype
Am I two halves of the same whole,
Or a player in the oldest story ever told
The child must destroy the father
But why bother
Now that I'm a father
With two beautiful daughters
Who both have brown names followed by browner names
So I will tell you as I told them
I come from brown and white
I come from left and right
My grandfather was right
When he said
Your father blessed you kid
By leaving you when he did

Posted August 2012, subsequently removed for editing

Poetic License

1.

I will tell you
he was my cousin
But actually he was my friend
I will tell you
we were half warrior on our fathers' side
Half poet on our mothers'
But if we are
who we come from
Then Manny
Was half postal worker
on his mother's side
Half mechanic
On his father's
While I was half unemployed
On my mother's side
Half remarried with a new family
On my father's

2.

When you are half brown
and half white
In a barrio—
Excuse me,
In a neighborhood
That is all brown
And your best friend
Is the darkest, brownest
Little boy in that neighborhood
Does he realize
That you love him
And envy him
At the same time

3.

Have you ever picked a fight
You know you can't win
We did
Many times
Manny did it to feel alive

I did it to feel anything

4.

There were two of us
And seven of them
(This much is true)
We threw bricks at them
Because they looked at us
With disgust in their eyes
(Actually we threw Slurpees,
Manny's was cherry,
Mine, a cherry/Coke suicide)
They were having a backyard barbecue
They were huge
They were white
They looked like members of ZZ Top
If those members of ZZ Top had been on steroids for years
They were members of a motorcycle gang
Not Hell's Angels
Nothing that dramatic
Or significant for that matter
They were outsiders
They were intruders
They were visiting friends they had in our neighborhood
So they were invited
But that does not change the fact
That they were intruders
(All true)
Manny stopped and looked at one of them
While he looked back at Manny
A chain link fence separated them
Warriors on both sides of a line
(Not so much a lie as poetic license
I knew Manny was a warrior
Had been a Golden Gloves youth boxing champion for years
But the bearded man on the other side
May have just been a weekend warrior)
"What are you looking at son?" He yelled.
"I'm not your son." Manny replied.
(Actually he didn't reply anything, he just let the slushee fly)
Instinctively I threw mine too
When they left our hands
They arched toward the outsiders like cold, red hand grenades
(Webster's dictionary defines hyperbole as a figure of speech in

which exaggeration is used for emphasis or effect)
In an instant they were over the fence
Two of them covered in red slush and ice
We stood our ground
Unafraid of repercussion
(Actually we both ran
And they gave chase)
After several blocks
A few of them gave up
But the other four
Ran like track stars
Ran like Jesse Owens
Ran like Michael Johnson
Ran like Ben Johnson
Ran like Usain Bolt
(Biggest lie so far, they did not run like track legends,
But they ran fast enough and far enough
That Manny and I chose to eventually stop and turn
And stand our ground)
They held us arms pinned behind our backs
While the two who were covered in red Slurpee
Took only a few swings at us, mostly body blows
They dropped us and as we gasped for air
They turned and walked away.
Manny looked at me and smiled.
I smiled back
Partly because the fear had left us as the air returned,
Partly because we were boys at war with the world,
And though we had lost this battle
We knew we had not yet lost the war.

A rough version of parts 1 and 2 posted September 2012,

Blasphemy

para Ethan, mi amigo de España,

for Ethan, my friend from Spain

It's 3 AM and I find myself walking through Jaén,
a small, but stunningly beautiful town in Spain.
I walk with four men, who are fantastically drunk,
but despite their stupor
they stop to point out the Cathedral
that is the very heart and soul of this small town,
and even though the darkness of night is upon us
the Cathedral is lit up by modern landscape lighting
revealing arches, columns, flying buttresses and the like.
I stare up at it
in awe of its sheer size
which is matched only by its beauty.
The four men
after several bars and twice that many drinks
have become more than my hosts
they have become my brothers,
and suddenly they are nowhere to be found.
In an instant, I find myself alone
surrounded on all sides
by silence
nightfall,
a sleeping village,
and the house of God.
Then, I see them in the distance pissing on the side of a house.
I realize at that moment
that I too have to urinate,
so I approach the wall where they stand
and unzip.
I say to the one nearest me,
who we all called El Presidente,
because he was the Principal of a local elementary school
"This house is ancient and beautiful."
"It is the home of our Bishop." He replies.
"Isn't it blasphemy to pee on a wall of the Bishop's house?"
"No, it's not. If we were pissing on the church
that would be blasphemy,
but pissing on the house of the Bishop is not.
It's not even a sin."
"How do you figure?" I asked, zipping up.

"The Man who lives in that house over there,"
he said pointing to the church, "is cool,
but the Bishop who lives in this house, is kind of an ass."

Found in a journal dated August 6, 2010, but posted September 15 2012

Mixtape Sonnets from the Year of Our Births

Subtitled

The De-evolution of Good Music

Dr. Martin Luther King Jr. said we should judge a man not by the color of his skin but rather by the content of his character. I believe this to be true, but I ask you, how should we judge a generation, by their actions, by their leaders? Maybe if we simply let their poets and artists speak for them, we can know if they are a more vibrant bloom than the generation before them or a fainter one. Maybe all we need to know about them, we can learn by listening to their music.

Me

"Maggie May" by Rod Stewart
"How Can You Mend a Broken Heart" by The Bee Gees
"Just My Imagination" by The Temptations
"Tired of Being Alone" by Al Green
"You've Got a Friend" by James Taylor
"Brown Sugar" by The Rolling Stones
"What's Going On" by Marvin Gaye
"Ain't No Sunshine" by Bill Withers

"Wild World" by Cat Stevens
"Won't Get Fooled Again" by The Who
"Love Her Madly" by The Doors
"Theme from Shaft" by Isaac Hayes

"Bridge over Troubled Water" by Aretha Franklin
"Proud Mary" by Ike & Tina Turner

My Wife

"Get Back" by The Beatles
"My Cherie Amour" by Stevie Wonder
"Only the Strong the Survive" by Jerry Butler
"Put a Little Love in Your Heart" by Jackie DeShannon
"I've got to be Me" by Sammy Davis Jr.
"Oh What a Night" by The Dells
"Something" by The Beatles
"Come Together" by The Beatles

"I Heard It Through the Grapevine" by Marvin Gaye
"Oh Happy Day" by The Edwin Hawkins Singers
"Hooked on a Feeling" by B.J. Thomas
"Hawaii Five-O" by The Ventures

"Love Theme from Romeo and Juliet" by Henry Mancini and His
Orchestra
"Proud Mary" by Creedence Clearwater Revival

My Oldest Daughter

"Smells Like Teen Spirit" by Nirvana
"Under the Bridge" by Red Hot Chili Peppers
"Remember the Time" by Michael Jackson
"November Rain" by Guns N' Roses
"This Used to Be My Playground" by Madonna
"Jump Around" by House of Pain
"Diamonds and Pearls" by Prince and The New Power Generation
"Don't Let the Sun Go Down on Me" by George Michael and
Elton John

"It's So Hard to Say Goodbye to Yesterday" by Boyz II Men
"Tennessee" by Arrested Development
"Set Adrift on Memory Bliss" by P.M. Dawn
"One" by U2

"Friday I'm in Love" by The Cure
"I'm Too Sexy" by Right Said Fred

My Youngest Daughter

"Believe" by Cher
"No Scrubs" by TLC
"Baby One More Time" by Brittany Spears
"Genie in a Bottle" by Christina Aguilera
"Livin' la Vida Loca" by Ricky Martin
"I Want it that Way" by The Backstreet Boys
"Wild Wild West" by Will Smith featuring Dru Hill and
Kool Moe Dee
"(God Must Have Spent) A Little More Time on You" by 'N Sync

"Man, I Feel Like a Woman!" by Shania Twain
"If You Had My Love" by Jennifer Lopez
"When You Believe" by Whitney Houston and Mariah Carey
"Every Morning" by Sugar Ray

"Kiss Me" by Sixpence None the Richer
"All Star" by Smash Mouth

Posted November 2, 2012

Sonnet for My Father

He says, "What you have to understand,
is your father was your model for God."

from Chuck Palahniuk's **Fight Club**

Perhaps it's true I turned my back on You
Because my father turned his back on me
I guess it's what some men are born to do
Father chose not to stay but rather flee
And this is how it is for some of us
Trapped between the absence and the silence
Not even a fleeting chance to discuss
My loyalty and your defiance
But I will pray and not be preyed upon
And look no farther than my true Father
Say goodbye now, let bygones be bygones
Not to forget but to forgive rather
After all these years isn't it odd
That you would be my model for God

Originally posted November 2012, subsequently removed for editing

Final Revision of Speaker for the Dead

for Newtown and the 20 children taken too soon

Tonight,
Let me be more than the words I recite
Tonight,
I'll admit I never really belonged to sunlight
Because my grandfather taught me,
Some things can only grow by the light of the full moon
So let these new stars in the night sky bloom
Let this be more than metaphor
Let this be sacred
Move this from elegy to exaltation
From song to chant
Form chant to cry
I want to scream to you back to life
Tonight I am you

All of you

At that age where you're more akin to God than men
20 angels among us masquerading as children
All of those beautiful little voices still reverberate in my head
Asking me,
Begging me,
To be their speaker for the dead
So this is not a poem
This is an act of desperation
This is hands cupped,
Breath soft,
On the glowing embers of your ashes
Hoping, praying that your spirit will rise
While the simple question of why blends into
How do I find the poetry in gunshots and lost lives?
So let night be day
Let tears be flood
Let this stage be your life
Let my ink be your blood
I want you to hear me
I want to write you all back from death
Let this be transubstantiation
I pat my heart three times
Because I believe in the miracle that I witness
So I pull out a page,

Clenching my pen with all of my might,
Trying to create just a little bit of light
In the middle of all this darkness
Desperate to write something beautiful and true
Something like each and every one of you
And it's true,
I know nothing of what it is to lose a son or a daughter
But these days I find myself feeling less like a poet
And more like a father
So I take a deep breath
Close my eyes just a bit
Think about my daughters' hands when they were six
But all I can manage to write is this,

Surely purple flowers sprouted from the bullet holes
In your bodies
Swaying back and forth like children dancing
At birthday parties

But that's just the poet in me talking again
And this cannot be about poetry
Because this is about a lost and violent youth
This is about an awful truth
And the truth is
The dead of night is still dark
The flood did come
But I couldn't write you an ark
My pen is filled with ink
This stage is nothing more than a dull wooden thud
And the only thing that poured forth from the holes
In your bodies that day,
Was blood
But know this,
When we
Speak of you
And we will often
From this day to our demise
In our words
Your spirit lies
And when we speak
You will rise
And in our voices
You become what you were
What you will always be
You become beautiful,

Innocent,
And free

Posted December 17, 2012

A New Twist On a Very Old Joke

There were 301 of us in the jury selection room at 8:15 AM on a Monday morning. After the judge swore us all in, he announced to the room that they only needed 90 of us for jury duty. Can you imagine that many people in the same room all wishing for the same thing at the exact same time, please dear Lord, don't let it be me? I can.

That's how we all felt in Ms. Smith's class that fateful day in third grade. Ms. Smith, who intimidated us all because we had never seen anything so tall, and blonde, and beautiful, in our lives. Ms. Smith who challenged us on the last day of every month with that ancient form of torture known as the spelling bee.

We all knew the drill, she would weed out the weak ones early with something difficult. The letter of the month was C. So we knew what was coming. Would it be "casualty" that made a casualty of one of us? Perhaps "catacomb" would send one of us to our final resting place.

She called the name of the student before the word. The chosen one who would have to approach the board and before everyone's eyes use the word in a sentence spelling it correctly or in most cases incorrectly for all to see. Your punishment for your transgression was to go and stand on the far wall, which we all jokingly called, el muro de la vergüenza, the wall of shame.

Ms. Smith's eyes scrolled down the attendance sheet looking for her first victim, I mean student. We all cringed. Our fists, our toes, our bowels tightened waiting for the blow. And then it came; Ms. Smith called the first student to the board with all the coldness in her voice of an Arctic vortex…"Jose!"

We were a classroom torn in two. All of us were at once thrilled that we were not chosen, but were all in fact heartbroken that little Jose was. He had only come to this country two years earlier from a small pueblo in Guerrero, Mexico, and though he had learned a great deal in a short time he was still struggling to grasp the language of his new country.

"Your word Jose is...consult" Ms. Smith stated.

Jose approached the chalkboard, retrieved the chalk with his small shaking hand. He looked up at the black board above him, as large and imposing as the night sky. Then using one hand to steady and calm the other, he wrote his sentence. We were all amazed by the first word, which was so large and perfect. Then we realized, he was using all caps, not on accident, but on purpose. At that moment Jose was living his life in all caps! His words filled the board, filled our hearts. His words filled the chalkboards of every classroom in that city that day, filled the hearts of every mocoso in that city that day. He was shouting to the world with his tiny piece of chalk. He was slapping Ms. Smith in the face with his words, slapping the faces of every Ms. Smith in the world with his words. When he stepped back to take it all in, he slammed the chalk back onto the tray, and smiled as he walked over to the wall of shame, not waiting for approval or disapproval. He was the master of his own destiny, and from that day on that wall would no longer be known as the wall of shame but rather the wall that Jose built with his words. We looked at Jose who stood there against his wall shoulders back, chin high, his smile was the Virgin's moon cresting ear to ear. Then we looked at Ms. Smith who looked at his sentence, her open mouth covered by her small hand. In that sentence was revolution, in that sentence was rebellion, in that sentence was retribution. With his words Jose had become Pancho Villa, Miguel Hidalgo, and Cesar Chavez. In those six words was their voice, was Jose's voice, was our voice.

Jose had sacrificed himself for us, had freed us, had saved us all with one simple sentence…

"*I LIKE MY WATERMELON CON SALT!*"

Posted January 7, 2013

Identity Issues

Two birds perched a low branch not far from the ground several feet below. Both dreamed of flying for the first time in their young lives. The first bird took a deep breath, took a step off the branch, and then took flight, spreading his wings and flapping majestically away. The second bird watched all of this happen. Then the second bird took a deep breath, took a leap of faith, and for the briefest of seconds he flew, and it was glorious, but after that first glorious second, he fell and plummeted to the grass below. He immediately righted himself and scuttled away. Why is it that some of us succeed while others fail? Why is it that some of us fly while others fall? Why did that first bird take flight and the second one could not? I'll tell you why...because that first bird was actually a bird, and the second one was a squirrel with identity issues.

Posted January 20, 2013, subsequently removed for editing

Likes and Dislikes

Joaquín

Likes finding wheat back pennies in his random change
Likes to reward himself with chocolate milk and chocolate
donettes
Likes fishing for catfish and though he has never tried it he thinks
he would like whittling a great deal

Dislikes mispronouncing words
Dislikes puppies, however cute they might be, licking the inside of
his ear
Dislikes people who hide behind keyboards

Aída

Likes butter
Likes collecting change in jars, but only nickels, dimes, and
quarters, no pennies, and saving it for a rainy day
Likes learning

Dislikes clutter
Dislikes movie trailers that reveal too much and ruin the endings
of films
Dislikes liars

Aiyana

Likes bike rides at night
Likes finding amusing videos on the Internet and showing them to
people for the first time
Likes eating her dinner one item at a time, saving what she likes
best for last

Dislikes cilantro
Dislikes people who talk during her favorite TV shows
Dislikes roosters crowing, alarm clocks, and all such early
morning things

Dakota

Likes hot tea and a good book late at night
Likes the sound her skateboard makes rolling across asphalt

Likes playing guitar and singing loudly whether anyone's around
or not

Dislikes when people don't listen when she has something to say
Dislikes the sound of a shirt rustling against her skin when
someone places their hand on her back
Dislikes mean people (dishonorable mention goes out to bugs
which she dislikes just a little less than mean people)

Posted February 1, 2013, subsequently removed and revised

Transubstantiation

I knelt beside him in the soil. I watched and listened as my grandfather closed his eyes and offered a prayer of thanks to his garden. He prayed in Spanish, years later I remember it in English.

My grandfather's garden was an oasis in the barrio. There really wasn't much to it. About 12 feet in length, less than twice that in width, but as a child I remember it as a place where I could hold magic in my hands. My grandfather knew just what time of year was best to plant tomatoes, potatoes, jalapeños, white and yellow onions, even the occasional melon.

I remember holding the seeds in my hand; they seemed so small, so insignificant. I think we all felt like that back then, small and insignificant. And even though I had seen it the year before and the year before that, I was amazed how with just the right amount of sunlight, water, soil, and prayer they would grow to feed us. Something large from something so small. Would we ever feel like that? On Sunday mornings the priest would change the wine into blood through transubstantiation. There was a sacred kind of magic in Father's hands. My grandfather had it to. Somewhere between my grandfather's hands and the soil is where the magic existed.

Posted February 2, 2013

Cesar Chavez Speaks During His 25-Day Hunger Strike

Day 1

I ate well last night
So you must know I begin this fight
With a belly filled with frijoles and fire
With a heart full of hope and desire
That this will all end peacefully
So I begin my sojourn
Not forlorn
But filled with the knowledge
That our destiny
Is greater than your ignorance
I need look no further
Than the back of my hand
To remind myself
That we will no longer be seen
As immigrants in our own land

Day 3

I hunger only for freedom
I desire not food but equality
In our fields
Our schools
Our barrios
Our camps
Our towns and cities
Our homes
Our leaders
Our country
We thirst not for water
We simply thirst for justice
And remember brothers and sisters
Before we find it in them
Let us first
Find it in us

Day 7

Are you listening America
It has been one week since I've tasted food
Can you tell me

What do the grapes on your table taste like
Sacrifice?
Pesticide?
Hopelessness?
Blood?
Sweat?
Tears?
Or do they taste like fear?
The fear that you
Will have to work the fields
That we do

Day 10

Can you hear us America
In the voices of your white children
If you wonder why so many of them
Have beautiful brown accents
It's because you pay us meagerly
Despite the fact that we work eagerly
To clean your home
And raise your children
As if they were are own

Day 13

We may be simple field workers
But we are far from simple minded
We see you
Not watching us
Waste away

Day 14

"I have not yet begun to fight."

Day 17

We seek only what's right
Not violence
Only peace
Only a piece
Of what every American wants and deserves
The dream lives in us
As it lives in you

Day 20

There are things out there
That cannot be foreclosed upon
That cannot be taken from us
What we want
What we demand
Justice
Compassion
Peace
Safe working conditions
Fair wages
The chance for a better tomorrow and the day after that
These are not requests
These are rights
And they are unalienable

Day 22

Young people
I ask you,
What will you do?
When your time here is done,
What will they say of you?
I challenge you
Implore you
Entreat you
To do more
To be more
Than you ever dreamed possible
Your skin is brown like the earth we work
But you are so much more than the color of your skin
You are the dreams of all those who came before you
Sus padres
Sus Abuelos
Y sus padres antes que ellos
Never forget
Their sacrifice
How they toiled under the sun
So that you
And your son
Would not have to

Day 24

A beautiful viejito once said,
"Just because I speak with an accent, do not think for one second
that means I dream with one too."
What more than this needs to be said,
I ask you.

Day 25

Let this not be the end
Let it begin
With a whisper
With one voice spoken to another
With a paper and pen
With your hand on the shoulder of your sister
Your brother
Your father
Your mother
With a shout
With a chant
With a cry
With a poem
Sing it to your children
As you hold them
Let it start with me
With you
With us
All that is right
Is within our reach
Within our grasp
Let us practice what we teach
Let this be more than just a dream
Dreams don't fill the bellies of hungry children
While our hearts soar
While our heads are in the clouds
Let us look down to our feet
Planted firmly in the reality of soil beneath
Let us praise the bountiful earth
Let us rejoice in our beautiful hands
Which are the color of the dirt we work
Knowing that only we have the fortitude, the strength to do so
Let us shout it from rooftops
The power of our voice
Will leave them no choice

So say it now,
Say it loud,
Say it proud
Let the sound we make be the thunderstorm that wakes them
Let our accents rain down on them
Shake them to their core
Until they shout no more
But even then we continue until our voices strain
Hundreds of voices
Thousands of voices
Millions of voices
Shouting to the world
What we have known in hearts to be true along
Dilo conmigo, mi gente
Say it with me, my people,
Sí, se puede!
Sí, se puede!
Sí, se puede!

A rough version of the first three sections posted March 31, 2013, subsequently removed for editing

Enough

Let there be some kind of Light in this
Let there be healing and reflection
Let there be regret in the notion that boys will be boys
The torturer learns his trade at home
It's in the fists of the abusive father
The tirade of the mother whose words
Slice deeper than razor blades ever could
So he would rather knock on smaller boys than wood
There has to be growth from all this destruction
It cannot all be for nothing
So let sticks be open fleshy arms
Let stones be seeds
This is the calm after the storm
The peace after the war
How many children have to die
Before we say no more
The line in the sand has been drawn
Our children stand on one side of it
Will you defend them?
Will you hear their pleas?
Will you embrace the beauty of the softly whispered *please*
It's time we stand up
Not for ourselves
But for those who are called odd, different, and weak
It's time we speak
There is power in numbers
And our voices are stronger than their anger
So tag every wall
Post it in the comments section
Say it to their faces
Let it be our mantra
Our one word psalm
Write it in black sharpie on both palms
With one word we can write the wrongs
Enough
Enough
Enough

Originally posted April 14, 2013, subsequently removed for editing

You Know You're Getting Older When

(Subtitled: Sliding Doors, Pennies, and How We Love Each Other)

Someone I admire greatly said to me you shouldn't just post your successes, but your failures as well, so people who admire your work will know you're human and humble and somewhat of an idiot at times, so here goes...

You know you're getting older when you find yourself at the self checkout lane at Kroger like I found myself this morning and you look down on the ground a few feet from where you're standing and see a penny staring back at you, and you think to yourself, "Holy shit, there's a penny on the ground and it must be mine! I mean who gets that excited over a damn penny? I'll tell you who, small children and people who are getting older. (Momma says I get to pick up any shiny penny I see!)

So back to the story, I have 17 items which is two more than I should have to be utilizing the self checkout lane and I'm using my own eco-friendly bags, so yeah I'm also "that guy" at the grocery store. Anyway I don't want to step away or even slow down scanning as I'm already getting dirty looks from the people in line behind me waiting to use my self checkout machine, so I decide in that moment to continue scanning while sliding my left foot out to scrape the penny along the ground toward me making it easy to pick up when I'm done. Well, in the act of stretching my left foot out I proceed to simultaneously hyperextend and pull muscles in all three of my middle toes on that foot, yes I said, all three!

So I find myself in a hotel room in Kansas City with a very sore foot and a slightly bruised ego, but this confession does feel good. Oh, and to the one person who gets to see me without a shirt on a regular basis, my wife, please know when you see the bruise on my left shoulder, you should know that the sliding doors to the Holiday Inn Express in Kansas City open slower than any sliding doors in existence, and uh…yeah…I walked into them.

Posted May 6, 2013

Caine is Able

for Caine Smith, an eleven year old warrior for peace

Caine, the most able boy I know
Dared to let his hair grow
Longer than most boys do
In the United State of Texas
He speaks for us
The weird ones
The ones with two moms
The ones who don't get invited to proms
The ones who are choked
By boys twice their size
How many angry mobs
Does it take to realize
That being odd
Is something we should all strive for
That different is what the world needs more
Than anything else
That boys like Caine shouldn't fear hallways and bus rides
The way parents of bullied children fear suicides
So this is for Caine
For every second of pain
He's been forced to endure
By children who are parentally poor

Posted May 17, 2013

First Hand Beauty

I'm sitting in a chair at a desk at Goodwill while my daughter, who has been rocking clothes from the thrift store long before the song, looks around. I just finished reading a chapter in Markus Zusak's, *I Am the Messenger*, that reminds me so much of my wife's mother and her relationship with church and her brother, that it moves me to tears. All the while near me a fleshy woman talks on the phone with her sister. There is so much soul and laughter and joy in her voice. Their conversation ends with, "Girl, now that's what I'm talkin' about...you know I love you...I'll talk to you later girl." In the distance a six-year old girl takes her flip-flops off and tries on high heels, her mother laughs and hugs her. By the books, an unruly boy is scolded so loudly and efficiently by a mother's voice, which sounds like it should emanate from a drill sergeant rather than the five foot one frame pushing the cart, that he shuts up instantly. The woman who was on the phone laughs, so do I. There is so much first hand beauty in this second hand store.

Posted May 24, 2013

With All Due Respect and Affection

My uncle 'Tino did not like being bothered when he was in his room, especially when he was in his room doing a paint by numbers. My uncle had studied art at a nearby community college years ago but had given up his dream of being an artist to get a job and help out the family. Now, he found refuge from the world by painting pictures of leopards grazing on grass, or a solitary owl in a tree. They were all paint by numbers, but you could only tell if you got right up on them, from a few feet away they looked like masterpieces, he was that good.

I knocked and quickly entered before he could refuse me with his usual, "Go. The hell. Away." I sat on the corner of his bed my legs still too short at twelve to reach the floor when I did. I sat their silently while he painted a tree branch with the precision of a surgeon covering the branch with a coat of brown which corresponded with the small number 7 on it. I waited silently, patiently for him to come to a respite from his work. And then after several minutes he stepped back to look at his half completed masterpiece. "What do you think mi'jo?" Mi'jo translates from Spanish slang to an abbreviated form of mi hijo, or my son. But figuratively it means my little one, or my darling little one. My uncles would never know how much it meant to me that they called me that, having never heard my father refer to me as his son. When your mother is a single mother in the barrio, all of your uncles become a father figure of sorts to you.

"I'm no Pedro Picasso, but I like it!" not knowing if I had intentionally or mistakenly displaced Picasso's first name making him for the briefest of moments a Latino contemporary of my uncle, he laughed with that loud, booming laugh that began somewhere deep inside of him that I remember so well and said, "You now, you're right, it's pretty good."

Uncle 'Tino, can I ask you a question?" "You just did." "What?" Not getting his joke at first, "Oh...that's a good one! Tío, (which I sometimes affectionately called all of my uncles) I had a question about girls." This stopped my uncle in mid-brushstroke. "Some of the guys at school, you know Gustavo and Jesús and Manny were having a conversation about what they called the birds and the bees. So I asked uncle Junior what he thought on the subject, and he said that girls and women are like delicate flowers...if you are gentle with them they will open themselves up to you. I'm not sure what that meant, so I asked him and he just laughed and tousled my hair and told me to leave him alone. So I wanted to ask you what he meant."

"Look mi'jo, it's time you learn two things: Number one, people who write in metaphors are called poets. People who speak in metaphors are called pendejos. And number two, don't listen to your uncle Junior. He's...and I say this with all due respect and affection...kind of an ass."

There's some things you should know about my uncle 'Tino:

1. He's very fond of the expression "I say this with all due respect and affection..." If those words came out of my uncle's mouth there's a very good chance that a fairly brutal and extremely funny insult would follow. I think he honestly thought saying the phrase, "I say this with all due respect and affection" actually absolved him of any wrongdoing, and he was genuinely shocked when people found his comment that followed offensive.

2. He was an artist. He loved art the way I love words. He was the

first person to ever take me to a museum. I remember on that first trip there was an exhibition of some woman from Chicago who had taken black and white photos her entire life, and they weren't discovered until years after her death when her children found them and the negatives in several large, dust covered boxes. I remember reading years later that eventually her grandchildren sold them for twenty dollars a box at a garage sale, and the man who bought them recognized the genius in them and preserved and restored them and now they're worth hundreds of thousand of dollars, perhaps millions. I remember one of the photos was of a young man standing on a street corner in a suit. His head tilted down and away from the sun so that you could only see part of his face. I remember thinking the man looked handsome, but sad. My Tío stared at that photo for several minutes before walking away. Now when I buy my wife and daughters a paint by numbers activity, which they all love, from Hobby Lobby, I like watching them when they work on them. Their patience and attention to detail reminds me so much of my uncle 'Tino.

3. He was the oldest and strongest of all of my uncles. Although my uncle Adolfo, Juanio, and Junior were all taller, and one of them, Adolfo, had a temper on him that was well known in the barrio of my youth, the one person he would never cross was his older brother 'Tino, who made up in girth what he lacked in height whenever taking down his little/big brothers.

4. He was a runner. He ran five miles every morning. Whether it was raining, sleeting, or one of those triple digit Texas summer days that was well into the upper 90's even as early as dawn, my uncle 'Tino would rise with the unforgiving sun and run. He always took such good care of himself, which made it that much more heartbreaking when he was diagnosed with cancer years

later. In the end he was merely a shell of the man who towered over me during those years when I was a child.

5. He was the only one of my mother's four brothers or four sisters to never marry. He talked to me only briefly about the occasional girl he dated in high school, but when he did he would describe them concisely like a journalist stripping the story of passionate active verbs, never bothering to assign adjectives to the nouns. They were always simply "girls," never "pretty" or "lovely." I also noticed that he described them only while painting never taking his eyes off the canvass, focusing more on the brush in his hand than the memory of them, and often he trailed off when talking about them like they were nothing more than a passing whim or a flight of fancy; it was as though none of them ever meant anything to him. In fact, in later years, no one ever really saw him with a woman. I remember this was something my tíos and tías used to whisper about when they thought I wasn't listening, but I was always listening. I don't know why. I think I just didn't want to miss anything, not even as a small child.

6. Of all my uncles, he was the one most like my grandfather, who raised me when my mother could not, and my father would not. He had an immeasurable strength, but he also had a compassion about him. He felt things deeply, but he was not quiet like my grandfather, who was as quiet as the earth he worked. My Tío was loud and more than a little rebellious. I think they were the antidote to one another my grandfather and my uncle. Most people thought they were as different as night and day, but I knew better. They both shared a compassion that was so deep it remains in me today, they both shared a name that my wife and I would pass on to our youngest daughter, and they both shared me. So I found that I spent most of my hours as young boy bounding

between my grandfather's silence and my Tío's rebellion.

7. My uncle 'Tino asked me once when I was quite young, "What do you want to be when you grow up?" "Poet." I replied. I didn't know back then where that answer came from or why I said it, but I knew I meant it. "Poet, huh? You now there's no money it, right." My uncle always asked questions like that, in declarative sentences. He looked at me with surprise and maybe even a little pride and said to me, "Now mi'jo I say this with all due respect and affection, but how you gonna' build house made of poems?" He said that to me. It has stayed with me always. "I don't know," I said with all the resolve of a rusty toy soldier. He put his hand on my shoulder and squatted down so as took look me right in the eye like he would do when he was about to say something he wanted me to remember. "So who's your favorite poet?" "I don't know," I answered. "Well, if you're going to be a great poet some day the first thing you have to figure out is the answer to that question." I have never forgotten that conversation with my uncle.

8. The only thing he loved more than painting was his beloved Dallas Cowboys.

9. If something you said (and by "you" I mean any of you, President, mixed martial arts expert, what have you) was bullshit, he would call you out on it, immediately and to your face. My Tío was once confronted by his younger brother as to why he was so harsh and brutally honest with people. I'll never forget what my uncle 'Tino said to this accusation. "I know sometimes the things I say rub people the wrong way, but what you have to understand 'mano is this, I don't give a rat's ass."

10. My wife, who my Tío only met on his deathbed when she was my fiancée, has so much in common with my Tío. For one, they are the only two people I have ever met in my entire life who love

using the expression, "I don't give a rat's ass." For this reasons and so many others I know if he were alive today exactly what he would say to me, "Mi'jo hold on to that woman. She's stronger and smarter than you. And I say this with all due respect and affection but when it comes to looks, on a scale from one to ten, she's somewhere between a nine and ten, and you mi'jo, well...you're not."

Originally posted June 2013, subsequently removed for editing

After It All

He said,
He loved her
Despite the fact that she
Was named after one of the four seasons
And now you're thinking
Was her name Summer or Autumn?
He said,
It doesn't matter
They're both the same person
And like both seasons
They always leave for all the wrong reasons.

Posted June 5, 2014, subsequently removed for editing

Familia Moderna

So we just finished watching an episode of Modern Family about dreamers and realist and how they're attracted to one another. My wife asked us each, "Are you a dreamer or a realist?" My girls weren't quite sure, so I made it easy for them, I asked, "Would you rather find a twenty dollar bill or a field of unusually tall sunflowers?" My wife immediately said, "Twenty dollar bill." I immediately said, "Field of unusually tall sun flowers." Both my daughters replied simultaneously, "A twenty dollar bill in the middle of a field of unusually tall sunflowers." This is what happens when a realist marries a dreamer, this is what happens when the sky meets the earth. This is my family. And I wouldn't have it any other way.

Posted August 1, 2013

Grill Joaquín, Grill!

Today, for no particular reason, I decided to go ahead and grill a little bit. So I grilled 16 hot dogs. And when I done that, I thought maybe I'd grill four chicken leg quarters. And when I done that, I thought maybe I'd just grill up five hamburger patties. And I figured, since I grilled this much, maybe I'd just grill two slabs of fajitas that my wife had marinating in the fridge for two days. And that's what I did. I damn near grilled everything in our fridge. For no particular reason I just kept on grilling. I reached clear into the bottom of the crisper drawer and I grilled some onions and peppers too. And when I done that, I figured, since I'd gone this far, I might as well turn around, and make some homemade salsa. When I got done with that, I figured, since I'd gone this far, I might as well just wash all the dishes and clean the grill and all the counters. So that's what I did.

Posted September 1, 2013

Homework

I have just finished my first reading of *Tuesdays with Morrie*. I say first, because I know I will return to this little, big book the way one returns to an old friend or a brother just to hear their voice again after a long absence. Perhaps my second reading will be out loud to someone I love. Now, I find myself on a plane on my way to speak with college students in Maryland about poetry and its role in my life. The person responsible for inviting me to this event saw me teach a writing workshop several months ago. He called me last week knowing that today was supposed to be a one hour performance of poetry and story telling, and asked me if I would be willing to just do 30 minutes of performance and then simply teach for 30 minutes, he would see to it that every student had a pad and pen to write with. I instantly said yes. Some days I feel more like a poet and less like a teacher, but after finishing this book I am feeling more like a teacher and less like a poet today. The book's ending reminded me of a time several months back when I bumped into an former student of mine, Collette, at a grocery store. She looked like a million bucks, all heels and power suit, and she told me how she had just finished grad school and how well her career was going, and how happy she was. I downplayed just how proud I was of her so as not to embarrass her, but I was/am so proud of her and all of my former students out there making their way in the world. This is a quote from the book, "A teacher affects eternity; he can never tell where his influence stops." Henry Adams said this, it's good, no? Well, I don't know if Adams was right, but I know this to be true: each and every one of my students affected me, your influence never stops. Thank you all. By the way, I still like to think of myself as your teacher, (even though many of you were/are smarter than I) so for homework, read *Tuesdays with Morrie*, for extra credit, read it out loud to someone you love.

Posted September 18, 2013

The More You Know

Everyone be careful this evening, remember if you're Charlie Chaplin tonight and your hat flies off, you instantly become Hitler.

Posted October 31, 2013

Kids Got It Too Easy These Days

So I just asked my oldest daughter to go pick up my youngest daughter from her sleepover, when she asked where is she at, I drew her a map and wrote her directions out to the side of said drawing. The instructions included the following:

When you cross Joaquín's creek (If Dawson can have one so can I damn it!) go around the bend just a shimmy, the first street around the curve just past the elementary school is called Bilbo or Babbins or something like that, turn right there; she is either two or three houses down on the right, the address is something, something, 09.

She looked at my map and said, this is the worst map ever. I'll just text her and ask her for the address and map it on my phone.

Two things about this exchange: 1. I don't care what anyone says, I have mad cartography skills. And 2. Kids got it too easy these days.

Posted November 27, 2013

The Sign Above the Assassin's Head Read, Hate

So there is a woman sitting across from me at Gate H8 at the airport. I judge her to be approximately 70 years old. She is wearing grey leather boots, grey leather pants, a lime green raincoat, and a scarf that has grey, lime, and blue swirled together in a dizzying array. She, like myself, is trying to bring style back to travel. Our eyes just met for the briefest of seconds, and in that short time, I swear they said to me, "The Fight Club T shirt is boss, but don't fuss with me, I once killed a man when Woodrow Wilson was President."

Posted December 3, 2013

Q and A

I spent the afternoon with eighth grade students at Chaparral
Middle School in Tucson today, and after I shared my story and
some poems with them, the Principal asked if I could stay an extra
ten minutes for a quick Q and A. I replied I would be honored.
What follows are some of the questions these eighth grade students
asked me:

"Have you ever felt a period of darkness in your life that seemed
unbearable and how did you get beyond it?"

"When you're trying to write and the words just won't come, what
do you do?"

"Have you ever had a situation in your life where you fear you
may have let your wife and daughters down?"

"What do you do when someone in your life lets you down? How
do you find a way to forgive them?"

These were just some of the questions...I have done Q and A's at
some of the most prestigious universities in the country and not
been asked questions that were as probing and heartfelt as these.

Here's a question and answer for all of you. How many poets do
find in the average middle school in the world? Too many to
count.

Posted December 6, 2013

Drowning Not Waving

The legend of la llorona
Is always told in the dark
It tells the story of a woman
With a broken heart
The story begins the way all stories start
With unrequited love
With the slightest shove
Her name is always María
His name is never the same
He is always depicted as cruel
And she is always the loveless fool
Who will do anything to keep her man
Even staining her hands
With the blood of her niño
If you listen closely late at night
You can hear her cries
Mi hijo! Mi hijo! Mi hijo!
She held her child under water
Because he didn't want to be a father
This is the horror in the story
It's the part that's meant to be gory
It's meant to strike fear in the hearts of the young
To keep them disciplined
To keep them near home
And here in lies the contradiction
How could a mother hurt her own children
But it's funny
How life can be stranger than fiction
I lived with a wailing woman
I was a small body floating down river
It took me years to forgive her
She held me down for so long
Not realizing just how resilient, just how strong
A child can be when he's forced to swim or drown
When he's forced to run or stand his own ground
My mother's name is María
His name was never the same
Was there a pregnant pause
Before she pushed me into the water
Did he even bother
To try and stop her
It's the hardest story a son can tell
That his mother's hands and his father's silence

Were all he ever knew of hell
I was a small body floating down river
My lungs filled with water
And words
With water
And hate
With water
And fear
The sounds of my mother's wails still echo in my ears
Mi hijo! Mi hijo! Mi hijo!

I was born of my mother's cries
And my father's lies

Her voice
And his silence

Her hands
And his eyes

He stands at her side
The last thing I remember hearing
Was her wailing
Mi hijo! Mi hijo! Mi hijo!
Calling me to return
The last thing I remember seeing
Was my mother crying
And my father frowning
They always thought I was waving
But I was drowning

Posted December 30, 2013, subsequently removed for editing

After Fruitvale Station

Before I was a writer and a poet, even before I was a teacher, I was a young man going to college who at the same time worked at a litigation service making copies for some of the biggest law firms in Dallas. It was merely a job, nothing more. But it helped put food on the table for Aída and me. That job helped us get through school, so I was appreciative and worked as hard as I could for them. I was made the youngest assistant manager in the company's history. And one day after leading a half-day Saturday shift, one of my team members offered a ride home to me and another employee. It's been so long, so many years, that I have nearly forgotten their names, but I think the young woman who offered me the ride was named Winnie, and I'm certain the young man, who was a great employee and always had a smile on his face, was named Troy. They were both African American, or Black. I was Mexican American or brown. So we all got in Winnie's truck and left downtown Dallas, laughing, acting a fool, and cutting up. Right as we pulled into Deep Ellum just off downtown the sirens flashed behind us, and two white Dallas Police officers pulled us over. When I asked them why, they said we had a cracked windshield, which Winnie did. The crack was about three inches in length in the upper right hand corner of the windshield. They asked Winnie to put both hands on the side of the truck and not move them one inch. They asked me and Troy to get out of the car and kneel on the sidewalk with our hands behind our heads. They made us take our shirts off. They searched the truck and found my backpack in the bed. One of the officers grabbed my pager from my side and held it in front of my face and asked me, "Are you a _____* drug dealer? Well, are you? Are you a _____* drug dealer?" I snapped at him at said "No!" Troy whispered for me to calm down, and not say anything. I looked over at him and he was crying. He was truly terrified. The sight of him crying calmed me momentarily and I knew at that moment I responsible for his life and mine. One of the officers grabbed my backpack and held it to my face and said, "What's in this? You a _____* drug dealer?" I replied "Ain't nothing in there but books." One of them reached into my back pocket and took out my wallet. He turned to his partner and said, "He's only got 40 bucks in here." I think at that moment I realized they were looking to get paid. As one of the officers dumped the contents of my backpack on the street, the other stood right behind me. I whispered something under my breath about what cowards they were, and the officer behind me said, "What did you say?" Troy turned to me and said, "Shut up, Joaquín." I told the officer, "I didn't say anything." He had his hand on his gun the entire time, but at that moment he pulled his weapon and placed the barrel to the back of my head and said, "That's what I thought." The other officer who had just dumped my textbooks on the street sifted through the contents of my backpack and motioned for his partner to head back to the squad car. They both walked slowly back to their cruiser and one of them yelled, "You get that windshield fixed soon." The other yelled, "You all have a nice day...be safe." Troy and I put our shirts on. I picked my things up off the street. We drove away, and none of us said a word. We just sat there in silence and humiliation and helplessness of it all. This is the first time I've written about this. We cannot allow young Black and brown men to be hunted and preyed upon. Oscar Grant III deserved better. Troy deserved better. We all do.

I will not defile my piece/peace with their hateful words. Their curses have been lifted/broken, and do not deserve to be written/spoken.

Posted January 15, 2013

Trinity

for Aída, Aiyana, and Dakota

I knew one Trinity as a child
the Father, the Son, and the Holy Spirit.
My tío Silastino once said to me after mass,
"A Trinity cannot exist without a woman.
Remember that mi'jo."
I always have.

When I was no longer a child and not yet a man
I knew one Trinity
My father, my mother, and my grandfather.
It wasn't any more
or less holy than the one I knew
as a child.

As a man I live with a Trinity
of women.
One of you sacrificed your flesh
to save so many,
one of you is no longer a child
but now a woman,
one of you said to me after class,
"My happiness cannot exist without you.
Remember that dad."
I always have.

To each of you and all of you
I say,
I love you. I love you. I love you.

Posted January 16, 2014

Poets are Liars and Thieves

1.

When I was nine years old
My cousin Jose dared me to steal a package of Kool Aid
From Jerry's Super Mercado.
So after purchasing 12 packets for a dollar
I took the small brown paper bag
Back to the rack they hung on
And placed one more in it.
As I walked out the door
I felt the hand of a giant grab my jacket from behind
And the store manager pulled me into the office
Where they cashed checks and made change
And called my grandfather.
I waited
And when he arrived
He shook his head
Looked at me
and said nothing.
He offered his apology in Spanish
To the store manager
Assuring him that this would not happen again.
We walked home in silence.
Later that night,
My mother spanked me in the bathroom for stealing.
When she exited, my godmother entered and spanked me.
When she exited, my godfather entered and spanked me.
None of them spanked me hard enough to be abusive.
All of them spanked me hard enough to never forget this moment,
And years later write a poem about it.
As my godfather walked out of the bathroom,
My grandfather entered,
He stood over me
Then realizing, I think, that he was looking down on me,
He sat at the edge of the tub
Shook his head and said nothing.
But in his eyes was all the sadness,
All the disappointment in the world.
I cannot tell you
How many times
I was spanked by my mother or godparents that day,
But I can tell you what my grandfather's eyes looked like
At that moment,

What the silence of that bathroom,
As he sat beside me,
Weighed in metric tons.

2.

A Latino student of mine once asked me about the derivation of
the prefix "mega." Knowing that he was the kind of student that
was mystified by origins, knowing that he was a C student
struggling to maintain his low C average, knowing that I was on
the verge of losing him, I looked him right in the eye, and said it
derives from the Aztecs. A bold face lie. I went on to tell him
they built monuments larger than most because their dreams were
larger than most. They word comes from them. So do you. This
is the first time I remember lying to a student to inspire them. It
would not be the last.

3.

To Jose, you owe me no apology for daring me to steal, because I
know now, thinking back on it, you were daring me to do so much
more, to take, to feel, to run, to risk, to burn, to dare, to dream.

To my godparents, I am not sorry for causing you to forget your
God.

To my mother, I am not sorry for lighting the fire under your rage
and I am not sorry for your sore hand.

To my students, that I lied to or didn't lie to, to inspire you, I am
not sorry. I'm not sure if you fact checked me many years later. If
you did, did you feel joy in knowing that I would compromise my
principles to encourage you? Or did you feel rage knowing that I
would do such a thing?

To my grandfather, to you, I am sorry, that I ever caused you to
feel the weight of my sins on your shoulders that had been
burdened already by the sins of so many others.

Posted only momentarily January 17, 2014, subsequently removed for editing

Somewhat Sonnet for Peyton Manning #1

1. Joe Montana
2. Terry Bradshaw
3. Troy Aikman
4. Tom Brady
5. John Elway
6. Ben Roethlisberger
7. Bob Griese
8. Jim Plunkett
9. Roger Staubach
10. Bart Starr
11. Eli Manning
12. Each of these NFL quarterbacks has more championships than Peyton Manning. 13. You could argue that Montana and Brady are as good or better than Peyton Manning, but in my estimation in terms of strength, endurance, accuracy, intelligence, and all other aspects that go into making one, Peyton Manning is the greatest quarterback to have ever played the game of football, and this is coming from someone who was born and raised in Dallas and worshipped Captain America (number 9) as a child. 14. Peyton Manning, who is the greatest quarterback of all time, does not have as many championships as these eleven quarterbacks. Omaha! Peyton Manning, who is the greatest quarterback of all time, does not have as many championships as his brother. Omaha! What does this say about Peyton Manning? Omaha! What does this say about football? Omaha! What does this say about me? Omaha! What does this say about any of us?

Posted January 18, 2014

Somewhat Sonnet for Peyton Manning #2

1. Peyton Manning, the greatest quarterback to ever play the game of football, comes from a long line of quarterbacks. 2. His younger brother Eli is the quarterback for the New York Giants and though he has less talent than Peyton he has one more world championship than Peyton. In The Bible, the sons of Eli are punished for their transgressions. Will Eli's sons play against Peyton's sons? 4. Peyton Manning's father was a quarterback for the New Orleans Saints for ten years. 5. Some might argue that he was the most gifted of the three, but never had the talent around him that Eli and Peyton had. 6. For years Archie Manning, who played football like Emily Dickinson wrote poetry, with quiet ferocity, had to watch his fans wear paper bags over their heads with the word "Aint's" written on them. 7. But oh, did you know that Eli and Peyton have a brother named Cooper? 8. Cooper once talked his two younger brothers into wearing the paper bags over their heads. A joke their mother did not find amusing. But despite his joke within the confines of his home, I'm sure he got into many fistfights at school defending his father's Saints. 9. He takes pride in being able to call himself the "other brother." 10. He takes pride in the fact that he gets to spend more time with his family. 11. In high school, Cooper's team won the state championship, and his senior year he caught 76 passes for 1,250 yards. Those passes were thrown to him by the new starting quarterback, sophomore, Peyton Manning. 12. I've heard to be a great quarterback you must be tight but loose, two words often used to describe Joe Montana. I've heard to be a great quarterback you must have the ability to be serious when needed and relaxed at other times. Peyton is serious. Eli is relaxed. Cooper is both. 13. His freshman year at Ole Miss, Cooper experienced numbness in his fingers and was diagnosed with a spinal injury and told he could never play football again. 14. What is it to be the son of greatness? What is it to be the brother of greatness? In the Manning household is the trinity observed the father, the sons, and the ghost of the greatest football player that never was?

Posted January 19, 2014

The Cost of Getting to the Next Gig

They were both young
and thin
and lovely
(most would use the word "beautiful"
to describe them
but I am a poet
who was born poor
which means I'm selective
with most things I use,
but especially words
and I reserve that word for only one woman)
I saw them while walking down Hollywood Boulevard.
The one sitting
beating the overturned
bucket with drumsticks
was white.
The one with the guitar in her hands
looked to be half white and half Black,
but looks can be deceiving.
She may have been all Black
or half Black and half a dozen other things.
But I know a Black poet
who can look at someone from Africa,
and guess what country they are from with great accuracy.
And since I am made up of two halves
I fancy myself someone who can see others like myself,
for the splendor of both halves that make up the whole.
They played a song by Cee Lo Green,
you know the one with the curse word placed brazenly in the title,
but they played the cleaner, radio friendly version of the song.
The crowd that gathered was large
and I truly believe they gathered
not because the two young women were attractive,
but because they were quite talented,
and although they failed to make the song their own
their cover was quite good.
As they played the last note everyone erupted in applause
but I was the only one to drop money in their bucket
a five-dollar bill
which is quite a lot for someone so selective with words
and other things.
I didn't drop the money in their bucket
because they were pretty.

(I refuse to ever do such a thing)
I didn't drop the money in their bucket
because of their performance.
I didn't drop the money in their bucket
because they were two young ladies,
and I am the father of two younger ladies.
I dropped the money in their bucket
because I am a poet
who has performed with a bucket in front of him,
and I know just how much a gallon of gas costs.

Posted January 19, 2014

My Money's on the Rhino

Corey Knowlton, a citizen of the great country of Texas, a place where you can buy shotgun shells and taco shells at any local Walmart won the right to hunt a black rhino in Africa, by outbidding all other hunters at the Dallas Safari Club recently. He lives in Hunt County. (You cannot make up irony like this; it seems in Texas irony is as abundant as big hair.) He has been threatened by other people with guns that if he chooses to go through with this hunt, that they will in fact hunt him down and kill him. I do not condone the hunting of black rhinos or white hunters for that matter, perhaps we could all put the guns down and simply let Corey take on the black rhino in hand to hoof combat, winner take all. Take it from a man who knows a thing or two about a thing or two, my money's on the rhino.

Posted January 19, 2014

Walt Whitman Reincarnated

I find myself
Sitting on a flight
Next to a baby
Or infant
I'm not quite sure
She is too young
To speak
But not too old
To know that one
Should not wail
On a flight
And Oh, Oh, Oh
How she wails
She wails in row 2
But it affects
The ears, and lungs, and hearts
Of every person sitting
In rows 1 through 20
Her lungs are Jimi Hendrix's guitar in the overhead compartment
Her lungs are a 747 engine
Her lungs are a thousand bags of carry on luggage
Filled with silverware
Dropped from 30,000 feet
And I think back
On both my daughters
As babies
Many years ago
How quiet they were
How many times people said to us on planes
Or city buses
Or park benches
They're such good babies
Perhaps some babies rage against silence
Because they don't understand silence
So naturally they fear it
They inherit this fear from their fathers
Who feared fields of wheat
Cotton balls
And all other such silent things
It seems harsh to say it
But these babies will likely grow up to be cowards
Like their fathers
They will grow up to be travelers who order room service

Because they fear
What others must think of them dining alone in restaurants
Perhaps I'm projecting
Perhaps poets with father issues are the worst judges of character
Perhaps I'm over thinking
Over analyzing
Over annoyed by the ringing in my ears
Maybe this small baby
Simply has a diaper filled with urine
Maybe this small human
Is hungry for her mother's breast
Maybe this small creature
Is Walt Whitman reincarnated
Sounding her barbaric yawp
Through the cabin of this plane
Because she
Like Walt
Like me
Like you
Just wants to be heard

Posted January 26 2014, subsequently removed for editing

Somewhat Sonnet for Black Rock Bands
Featuring a Guitar Solo by Brittany Howard

Robert Johnson
Bo Diddley
Jimi Hendrix
Bad Brains
Living Colour
Lenny Kravitz
Sevendust
Bloc Party
When asked what is your ethnic make-up? Brittany Howard the
lead singer of Alabama Shakes replied, "Mom is white, dad is
Black." The follow up question was, what do you identify
yourself as Black, white, or mixed? She replied, "I'm both.
Everything and nothing." Believe me girl, I've been there before.
TV on the Radio
Bad Rabbits
Earl Greyhound
Gary Clark Jr.
The Bots
Alabama Shakes

Posted January 27, 2014

Responsibility

So my wife has not one, but two coupons good for two dollars off a 24 pack of double roll, three-ply, Cottonelle toilet paper and she wants two packs, because when it comes to TP my wife don't play. So I'm in line at Walmart with two giant packages of toilet paper, one under each arm struggling to grasp these toiletry monstrosities because I'm merely a human and not an octopus, when I look over and notice in the line across from me a ten year old African American child is looking at me, then out of nowhere he cracks up laughing. Then out of nowhere so do I. Because I know the mind of a ten year boy, I had one once. My wife says sometimes I still do. I'm laughing because I know he's thinking, "Damn man, how many asses are you responsible for?"

Posted January 27, 2014

Full Court Prayer

The same week I found out that Pope John Paul II was named an Honorary Harlem Globetrotter was the same week I was asked to spend a few days at a Catholic High School teaching writing workshops that focused on poetry. During one of those days I was asked if I would like to attend a Mass in the middle of the day with freshmen students in honor of Catholic Schools Week. Before I answered I was told the Mass would be held in the school's basketball gym. Considering I was raised one half Catholic on my mother's side and one half shooting guard on my father's, of course I said yes.

1.

In November of 2000, 50,000 people gathered to see the Pope have this Harlem honor bestowed upon him.

2.

In April of 2003, 20,000 people witnessed Michal Jordan's final game as a basketball player.

3.

What must the masses gathered in Saint Peter's Square have thought of the Pope holding this red, white, and blue basketball in his hands, how odd he must have looked?

4.

What must the fans that night have thought of Jordan draped in the navy and white of the Washington Wizards and not the red and black of the Chicago Bulls, how odd he must have looked?

5.

But oh, did you know that the Pope was not the only one to receive such an honor, no, Pope John Paul II and Reverend Jesse Jackson were named the seventh and eighth honorary Globetrotters that day.

6.

Yes, it's true. The statue of Jordan outside The United Center, reads "The best there ever was. The best there ever will be." But did you know that at Gate 7 there is a bust that is stunning in its scope, nuance, and representation of Scotty Pippin, who many consider the greatest complimentary player to have ever lived. Best ever, yes, it's true Jordan was the one among a merely human bunch, but it didn't hurt that Pippin was the two, in their Chicago one-two punch.

7.

The list of Honorary Harlem Globetrotters include:

Pope John Paul II
Henry Kissinger
Bob Hope
Nelson Mandela
Whoopi Goldberg
Jackie Joyner-Kersee
Jesse Jackson
Kareem Abdul-Jabbar

8.

The list of the greatest basketball players of all time include:

Michael Jordan
Koby Bryant
Oscar Robertson
Tim Duncan
Magic Johnson
Larry Bird
Wilt Chamberlain
Kareem Abdul-Jabbar

9.

The announcement of the starting five for the Honorary Harlem Globetrotters would sound like this:

At point guard, from The University of South Africa, a 6-0 guard, number 27...Nelson Mandela

At shooting guard, from the Boys Industrial School for Troubled Youth, a 5-10 guard, number 4...Bob Hope

At small forward, from UCLA, a 5-10 forward, number 63...Jackie Joyner-Kersee

At power forward, from Jagiellonian University, a 5-10 forward, number 3...Pope John Paul II

And at center, from UCLA, a 7-2 center, number 33...Kareem Abdul-Jabbar

10.

The announcement of the starting five greatest basketball players of all time would sound like this:

At point guard, from Michigan State University, a 6-9 guard, number 32...Magic Johnson

At shooting guard, from North Carolina, a 6-6 guard, number 23...Michael Jordan

At small forward, from Indiana State, a 6-9 forward, number 33...Larry Bird

At power forward, from Wake Forest, a 6-11 forward, number 21...Tim Duncan

And at center, from Kansas by way of The Harlem Globetrotters, a 7-1 center, number 13...Wilt Chamberlain

11.

On April 2, 2005, after dedicating the bulk of his life toward the service and salvation of all whom he encountered, Pope John Paul II died of heart failure.

12.

On April 16, 2003 after dedicating the bulk of his life toward the game of basketball, Michael Jordan played in his final game. How many hearts were broken that night?

13.

Stat Sheets:

Pope John Paul II:

Auxiliary Bishop of Kraków, Poland (1958-1964)
Titular Bishop of Ombi (1958-1964)
Archbishop of Kraków, Poland (1964-1978)
Cardinal-Priest of San Cesareo in Palatio (1967-1978)
Ordained Pope and Head of the Catholic Church (October 16, 1978-his death April 2, 2005)
Proclaimed venerable by his successor Pope Benedict XVI (December 19, 2009)
Beatified after the Congregation for the Causes of Saints attributed one miracle to him, the healing of a French nun from Parkinson's disease (May 1, 2011)
A second miracle attributed to him was approved and confirmed by Pope Francis two days later (July 4, 2013)
Pope John Paul II will be canonized (April 27, 2014)

Michael Jordan:

Olympic Gold Medalist (1984, 1992)
Sports Illustrated Sportsman of the Year (1991)
Leading Vote Getter- NBA All-Star Fan Balloting (1987, 1988, 1989, 1990, 1991, 1992, 1993, 1998)
College Player of the Year (1983, 1984)
College First Team All-American (1983, 1984)
Winner of both NCAA and NBA Championships
29 Career Triple Doubles
840 Consecutive Games of Double Figure Scoring
Scored 50 or More Points 37 Times
Scored 60 or More Points Five Times
Fourth Player In History to Win a World Championship and a Scoring Title in the Same Season
Named One of the 50 Greatest Players in NBA History

14.

I dreamt last night that my father and I watched as the game between the Honorary Harlem Globetrotters and the greatest basketball players of all time was tied going into triple overtime.

Shall we pray before and after the game?
Is nothing more sacred than one on one?
Can we find God in the joy and the pain?
Is nothing more kindred than father and son?
Can God be found in the hoop or the net?

Does He live between the reason and rhyme?
Father, was I your joy or your regret?
Did you play this game of ours all the time?
Did you play until day gave way to night?
Did you follow through, make a perfect arc?
Was I all that was wrong, or all that was right?
When you blocked me out, did it break your heart?
If it did, was it a slow or fast break?
There's a free throw line between love and hate.

Posted January 28, 2014, subsequently removed for editing

The Center Point Between the Two

My tío told me once that Centerville, Texas, gets its name by being the center point between Dallas and Houston. Which seems like an incredibly insignificant fact to name ones town after, but Centerville means so much more to me.

I45 is the interstate that links Dallas and Huntsville, Texas. That stretch of freeway is flat and long and unforgiving. Between the heat of the asphalt and the speed traps scattered from Palmer to Conroe, there is a great deal on that stretch of highway for a viejito and his grandson to be weary of.

My grandfather and I made the journey from the barrio of my youth to Huntsville twice a month for as long as I could remember. If you find yourself in Huntsville, Texas, you are likely one of two things: a student at Sam Houston State University or an inmate in Huntsville State Penitentiary. We went to visit my tío, my grandfather's son, and let's just say he was not a student.

My tío murdered his beautiful wife Rosalinda, there is no poetic way to say this. In fact, there is no other way to say this. So we made the drive partly for him, years later I would realize it was partly for us as well.

My grandfather drove a 1946 Dodge truck. Its color was somewhere between rust and primer grey. The truck had no AC, no heater, and no radio. My grandfather was one of those Latinos who thought if the posted speed limit was 60 miles per hour, it was a good idea to do 50. Picture that drive during the summers of my youth. 100-degree heat. No AC. No radio. To say the drive was long was to say Robert Johnson played guitar well. There are understatements and then there's the drive to Huntsville in my grandfather's truck.

My grandfather was a silent man, always thoughtful. Always thinking before speaking. In every action, in every word spoken or unspoken there was thought behind it. So the drives from Dallas to Huntsville were not only long, they were usually quiet. The sound of asphalt rolling under our tires. The sound of wind blowing past my outstretched hand.

There wasn't much to see on the drive, the occasional junkyard, farms, flat land as far as the eye could see. But when you reach Centerville, Texas, for no reason at all a pine forest sprouts up on both sides of the freeway and leans over you like giant green monoliths. It stretches for miles. And it was just then, when under the shade of those pine trees, that my grandfather would start to sing. He would sing corridos, these ancient Spanish folk songs about men who lived epic lives. Men like Pancho Villa, Miguel Hidalgo, and Joaquín Murrieta. He would sing softly under his breath, perhaps thinking that the roar of the freeway under us would mask his voice, but I would lean over toward him just an inch or two so as not to arouse suspicion, but close enough to listen to his beautiful, ancient voice, deep and dark as well water. I'll never forget that voice.

If you ask me today, I cannot tell you the color of the mortar that formed the walls of that prison rising up from the earth. I cannot tell you how many armed guards were stationed in each tower as we exited the freeway and turned in to the prison grounds. I cannot retrace the path from the sign-in desk to the visitors' area for you like some cartography child prodigy, but I can tell you everything about my grandfather's voice, those songs he would sing, and those pine trees leaning over us surely to listen in as well.

Don't you see, this is what my grandfather did for me. This was his magic. He took what should have been the ugliest moments of my childhood, and through his voice he transformed them into the most beautiful. And no greater magic can exist.

My grandfather and I lived in the barrio that fell under the shadows of downtown Dallas. My tío lived in a prison made of colorless walls and barbed wire. Somewhere between the two was a pine forest that leaned in to hear the stories and songs of passers-by. My childhood was made up of so much ugliness and so much beauty, and I was the center point between the two.

Posted January 29, 2014

Women of Monsters and Men

When you are the other half
of a woman
who was broken
by the man
who was supposed to protect her from monsters
you come to know
that she will grow
into a woman
who values two things
above all others
her voice
and her choice
so when she chooses to speak of the past
and your first instinct is to ask,
why
take my advice,
shut up
for the briefest of seconds
and imagine the weight of the world
on the shoulders
of a small girl
whose father
tried to soil her flesh
to ruin her manners toward God and men,
and then
you will know what to do
for then
you will see that little girl as your daughter
you will see that little girl as you
you will close your eyes
take a deep breath
and wait patiently
for the weight of it all
to be lifted from her
and given to you
and you will know
that the choice you are given
is to question
or to listen
and the answer
will come to you in the silence that follows

Posted January 30, 2014

For the Birds

Surely you know
That not long ago
Two white doves released by the Pope
From his balcony window
Were instantly attacked by a gull and crow
Brutal and vicious said the Huffington Post
Yet, this battle of life and death
Of good and evil
Began as a gesture of peace
But oh,
Did you know,
Both doves managed to escape the attack and get away
And though one flew in a broken way
He flew nonetheless
Both winging their way from the violence that day
And now,
Surely you must think it blasphemous of me
To use both internal and end rhyme
To besmirch the Papistry
To describe the Vatican with words like vicious and violent
But you must understand
In this instance
I speak not as one who has tasted the body and blood
In this instance
I speak for the doves
I speak for the crows
Good is white
Bad is black
And so the story goes
But oh,
Did you know
That the two doves were not released by the Pope
No, in fact,
On that day two small children,
A boy and a girl,
Selected no doubt for their purity and innocence,
Released the doves into all that violence
What will the weight of this be on their souls?
Witnesses said the small boy openly wept
And had to be consoled
By the Pope who embraced him and patted his head
Assuring him all would be right with the world
All the while

The small girl
Laughed hysterically
Silly girl
Sad boy
Full of pain
Full of joy
From up above
They look below
One cries for the dove
One laughs for the crow

Posted January 31, 2014

It's the Little Things

A beautiful Puerto Rican woman said to me once, you can't just post your victories, you have to post your failures too. So I promise you, I will try to be as gentle with this post as possible. So I'm in Oregon with Aida and Natasha yesterday and we have eaten a LOT of very good food throughout the day and evening. (Actually I have eaten a LOT, they have eaten the normal amount that a human should consume...natty you gonna' finish that fish? Yes I will take extra Tabasco sauce on those fries...this has been my day so far.) So we find ourselves in a Safeway grocery store at 10 PM looking for snacks...my idea. When out of nowhere I feel a rumbling down in the deepest darkest depths of Dante's seventh circle of my stomach. So I excuse myself from the ladies and proceed to quick walk the inner perimeter of the Safeway looking for a bathroom, but to no avail. I'm beginning to panic. I approach the ladies and while doing the foxtrot side step dance with evident discomfort on my face, I throw Aida the keys to the rental car and say, "I have to run the two blocks back to the restaurant, I have a situation going on." As I run out the door I hear Natasha laughing louder than I've heard her laugh in years. So I'm running full speed across the parking lot of Safeway in the Oregon rain, while wearing a Fight Club T-shirt hoping that no young rapscallions will take me up on Tyler Durden's offer because if a ninety year old Sonny Listen hits me in the stomach at this exact moment, I will lose this fight in the most inglorious of ways. So I reach the restaurant and rush into the bathroom and find myself in a classic good news/bad news scenario. Good news, the stall is empty, unlocked and in good working order. Bad news, there is a 22 year old college student, who I judge to be named Zack by his haircut and Vans tennis shoes, in the bathroom as well. Well, as bad as I want to sit down, I fear when I do an explosive sound will ensue. So my foxtrot in that stall transforms into the saddest, most pathetic electric slide in history, as I'm desperate for Zack to clear out of the bathroom so I can do that voodoo that I do so well. Finally as he steps away from the urinal, rather than wash his hands and exit immediately, I can hear that he has chosen to pull out his phone and check his Facebook status. I can wait no longer. And I sit, and the sound that issues unto the universe from me is volcanic in its decibel level and duration, to which Zack says loudly, "WOAH! Dude that was a good one!" I was mortified, and regressed into the silence of the stall. At that point Zack approaches the stall door slowly and I hear him just outside the door merely inches from it, and with the gentleness of a priest offering absolution through a confessional door, he whispers,

"Come on man, it's okay to laugh, remember dude, it's the little things." At this point I erupt in laughter and Zack exits, and I hear him saying as he walks away from my life, "Cool, dude...cool." In my life, whether I'm traveling with my wife and sister, or at lunch with an artist from Vancouver, or in a bathroom in Corvallis with a college student I find myself surrounded by so much truth, and wisdom, and poetry.

Posted February 14, 2014

Note to Self

If this has taught us anything, it has taught us that everyone is desperate to be known. But only when one comes to know himself and accept himself for all his fragile complexities, for all his beautiful strengths and even more beautiful flaws, then and only then can anyone truly come to know you.

Posted February 16, 2014

.

Fairies from Fireflies

for Aiyana, who believes in love and fairies

I sat in a crowded cafeteria at a university yesterday, as I was there
to share poems with students. A place to sit in the cafeteria was
hard to find as students outnumbered the chairs significantly.
Finding my seat at a small table in a far corner was perhaps dumb
luck or fate or both. Next to me on one side was another small
table, sitting on one side of it was a young female African
American student; she couldn't have been more than 20. The chair
across from her and the chair across from me looked to be the last
two contestants in this game of musical humans. A young Latino
student carrying a tray and his hopes around like a lost and weary
traveler walked by both our tables several times sizing both of us
up. Then after a couple of minutes he approached the young lady.
I was happy he chose her rather than me, I could see in his eyes he
wanted to sit with her, but he was intimidated by the book she had
open on the table and her loveliness. Young man, I too have been
there before, intimidated by a woman who was smarter, stronger,
and more beautiful than I could ever hope to be. Perhaps that's the
story of my life so far. He asked her, "May I sit with you and eat
lunch, there are no seats anywhere. I promise I won't bother you
while you read." She replied, "Sure." He smiled at her and then
caught himself. She spoke first, "My name is Tranisha, (I smiled
at the thought of my niece who shares her name), what's yours?"
"Jose." "So Jose, are you a student here like me?" "Yes, but
today I'm on campus tutoring." "What do you tutor?" "Spanish
and French." Then something extraordinary happened, she asked
him a question in the most beautiful French I've heard in years.
His eyes lit up. He answered her. I was even more astounded by
his French; it sounded as deep and murky as the Seine. In his
voice was the sound of Paris I remember that summer so long ago
with my wife when we walked along Champs-Élysées hoping to
get lost in the beauty of that city. They talked, the two of them, in
French for 20 minutes. I picked up something about her falling in
love with the language in middle school and studying it all through
high school and her first two years at university as well. They also
talked about what they were studying and what they hoped to do
with their lives. At least I think that's what part of the conversation
was about. Right before I got up to leave, she asked him in
English, "So do you do anything else besides tutor and eat lunch
with random strangers?" "Yes, I work at Aztlán Cafe." "What's
that?" she asked. "I know it sounds fancy, but we just sell burritos
and bowls. But we use fresh ingredients and have several healthy

options. If you like we can exchange numbers and I can call you while I'm working and you can come in for burrito on the house." She thought for a second, her head tilted slightly to one side, and then handed him her phone asking him with her smile to create a new contact. The smile on his face as he typed his number into her phone was radiant. I swear it could have eclipsed the sun. As I got up and walked away from them, leaving them to the chaos and sounds of the most crowded cafeteria on the planet, the poet in me couldn't help but wonder, what if this is the beginning of their story. What if many years from now they tell their beautiful mejiafricana daughter the story of the day they first met and spoke French to one another for hours on end, losing track of time and the day, and for the briefest of moments the crowded cafeteria of the largest university in Oklahoma became L'Arpège. I smiled at the thought, thinking surely that's just the poet in me again creating fairies from fireflies...but then again...who knows? Maybe the only thing one needs to find love is a crowded cafeteria and the courage to ask a pretty young woman for a seat.

Posted April 5, 2014

What follows is an excerpt from Joaquín's forthcoming collection of short stories, *Fight or Flight*. Look for it in the fall of 2014.

Second Sight

When Juan was seven years old, he spilled a bowl of cereal on the new carpet in the living room. Juan's mother worked the night shift as a cocktail waitress at the It'll Do Bar. She met Juan's stepfather there. Juan's stepfather, Luís, was a drunk. Not the kind that hugged you too much and told you just how much they "loved you man." No, Luís was the kind that put lit cigarettes out on you, so when Juan spilled that cereal, Luís rose from his recliner, staggered down the hallway toward the coat closet, and returned to the living room with his aluminum baseball bat. Luís turned to face Juan, who was frozen with fear as any seven year old would be. Luís pulled the bat back over his right shoulder, closed his eyes, and swung for the fences. When he opened his eyes, Juan was unconscious on the ground, bleeding from both eyes and his nose.

Luís, despite his stupor, realized what he had done and fled through the front door into the darkness. When María, Juan's mother, returned home from work hours later it was she who called the ambulance.

The doctor told María that if Juan had immediately been rushed to the hospital the diagnosis might have been different, they might have relieved the pressure to the optic nerve with steroids and orbital decompression, but María who got off work at midnight found her son several hours after the brutal attack, and by then there was nothing anyone could do.

María imagined that Luís returned to Mexico where he had family. She never forgave herself for bringing a monster into her child's life. She never saw Luís again, and little Juan never saw anything again after that day.

Traumatic optic neuropathy, that's what the doctor called it, but what all those syllables meant to Juan was that the last thing he would ever see in his life was a man drunk with rage and whiskey swing a baseball bat at his face.

Growing up young and Latino in the barrio of the lower east side is as hard as it sounds, but when you're blind, young, and Latino it goes from being difficult to what Arturo, a neighborhood friend described better than anyone could, "Young, brown, and blind...damn vato you got triple trouble!"

Juan, who was only seven when he discovered just how dark this world could be, had a saving grace though, actually seven of them, his uncles. When you're a young Latino growing up in the barrio being raised by a single mother your uncles all become a sort of second father to you. Never was this more evident that in Juan's case.

When María and Juan returned home from the hospital she called all of her brothers, many of whom still lived in the neighborhood and asked them for two favors concerning Juan. Phone call after phone call through her tears she made each of them promise to help her with Juan knowing that most had children and responsibilities of their own to tend to.

The requests were simple, "Don't ever let him feel sorry for himself. And don't ever let him give up." That was all she asked. Each agreed they would do their best to help in whatever way they could. And though they all lived up to their word, one of Juan's uncles, the only one to never marry and have children of his own, Alejandro, Juan's oldest uncle who Juan affectionately called, Al, took this request to heart the most.

Only two weeks after his return from the hospital, Al stood over Juan's bed at six in the morning.

"Wake up. Juanito...wake up!"

"Tío Al, is that you?"

"Yeah. Okay you know I run every morning, right.".
Questions asked with declarative sentences, a trait common in all
of his uncles.

"Yes, I know," Juan said rolling over and pulling the blanket
over his head.

"Well, I'm not feeling like a run today, only a walk, not my
usual five miles only a mile or two, and you're gonna' walk it with
me."

"Don't be crazy tío, I'll trip and break my neck...I'm going
back to sleep."

Tío Al pulled back both covers and a sheet with one sweep
of his arm. "I'm sorry mi'jo I'm not asking, I'm telling." He
grabbed Juan by the sleeve of the T-shirt he was wearing. It was
his favorite T-shirt partly because of the fact that it had a picture of
John Travolta dressed in his white suit from Saturday Night Fever
on it, one hand on hip, the other pointing to the sky in that famous
dance pose of his, and partly because Travolta was a Juan like him
and his Abuela who died a year earlier had told him once that all
Juans are one half loco and one half magic. But what truly made it
his favorite T-shirt was the fact that it was an old faded iron-on,
and he could tell by the way it felt rough against his fingers when
he touched it, that it was in fact his favorite shirt without asking
anyone to prove it so with their sight.

Earlier in the year his uncle started reading The Adventures
of Huckleberry Finn with him. Juan loved the book because he
felt that he and his uncle and Huck and Jim were all cut from the
same cloth. Like Huck, tío Al was a prankster who loved to laugh,
but he was also ever watchful and constant like Jim. Juan
remembered reading a part in which Huck is described as a realist.

You know, to Huck, seeing is believing. Sitting up on the edge of his bed, his fingers rubbing against the rough iron-on that had been washed too many times and was beginning to peel off at the corners, Juan realized just then that now to him, feeling was not only believing, it was the closest thing to seeing a blind child could ever hope for.

Begrudgingly Juan stood up and put on the shorts and socks that his uncle had laid out for him and the tennis shoes that were under his bed.

"How is this going to work? You do know I'm blind, don't you?"

"I'll tell you how it's going to work, with less questions and more listening, so do me a favor, shut up."

"I don't ever remember you being this rude to me when I could see."

"I'm sorry mi'jo, shut up please. Now you are going to grab my right elbow with your left hand, like this." He placed his nephew's hand on his elbow. "We will walk together, you will walk just to the right of me and just behind me. It will be my responsibility to tell you when to step down or step up, slow down or stop. It will be your responsibility to listen and commit some of the things you experience to memory. Trust me, over time you will be able to walk this neighborhood on your own. We will walk every morning and some evenings as well. Some nights I'd like us to walk very late in fact, the way I figure, if you have to do this in darkness, so do I."

The walks were difficult at first. Al was slow and methodical, always pointing out new bushes that were planted, fallen tree limbs, knocked over trash cans, a crack that might trip Juan up, anything that might get in his way for that matter. The first route they walked was down several blocks through the park and to his elementary school, and then back. They walked that route for about two months, day and night. Al always challenging Juan to remember sounds associated with certain street corners, the smell of the taquería a few blocks down, placement of trees and play ground equipment, the number of steps that led up to the front door of the barrio elementary school. Juan was a diligent student always listening, always touching, always taking mental notes of things. Then one morning after making it to the front door of the elementary school like they had done a hundred times before Al sat on the steps with Juan in silence. The sun was rising over the city, the morning air was still cool.

"I'm having problems remembering."

"Remembering what mi'jo?"

"What colors look like. Ask me what black looks like and I can tell you that. But my memory of brown and green and other colors is starting to fade. I don't want to forget."

His uncle reached into both his coat pockets pulled out two things, a knife from one, and an orange from the other. He cut the orange down the center and handed half to Juan.

"Mi'jo smell it." Juan held the orange flesh to his nose and inhaled. "That is what the color orange smells like. Put out your hand." Juan held out his hand fingers spread, palm to the sky. Al squeezed his half onto Juan's palm. "That is what the color orange feels like on your skin. Now take a bite from your half." Juan did. "That Juanito is what the color orange tastes like. So tell me about the color orange."

Juan took a second bite before speaking, "It's light. Sticky. Sweet. It's kind of pretty like a sunrise. Yeah, it's kind of like a sunrise."

"Exactly mi'jo...exactly." Al stood, stretched a bit and turned to look at Juan still sitting there. "Look mi'jo, you know how we've been working with the walking stick lately."

"Yeah, I'm not so good with it."

"You're better than you think." His uncle had even taken to calling him, Obi Juan and the walking stick his light saber. "Look, you know the route home better than I do, every turn, every curb, every tree. You're ready, you've been ready for a long time. Here, take this." Al placed the folded up walking stick in his nephew's hands. "I'm heading home. I'll make us some eggs. I'll see you when you get there."

"How am I supposed to do this!"

"If all else fails...use the force Obi Juan."

"What are you talking about tío?" But it was too late, his uncle had already started walking the route back home. Juan could hear his uncle's footsteps, first against the sidewalk and then cutting across the grass. He kept shouting "Tío, don't leave me please, Tío come back!" How hard it must have been to hear those cries and not return to them, but Al ever the faithful uncle kept walking. Juan began to cry but quickly wiped his tears away as fear gave way to anger. Anger at his uncle quickly turned to anger at his stepfather, Luís, which quickly turned to anger at the world, but it was this anger that gave him the resolve to rise. He stood and frantically made his way back up the steps to the front door of the school, a buoy in a sea of darkness.

Juan remembered it was seven strides to the first step down and 18 steps down to the concrete pavilion that was home to the school's flagpole. He recalled that the flagpole was located exactly in the center of the courtyard. He remembered that his uncle laughed once and said, "Man, God must have been feeling very unpatriotic because it looks like one side of this flagpole was struck by lightening. There's a huge dent in it." Actually the dent looked as though it had been made by a baseball bat swung by one of the mocosos of the neighborhood no doubt, but Al wasn't ready to use the word baseball bat in front of Juan.

Juan remembered what his uncle had said to him, "If you ever get disoriented, remember just make it to the flagpole, feel for the rope ties on both sides. They're about the height of your head. In between the rope ties on one side of the pole is a huge dent, follow the concrete path on the side with the dent toward the sidewalk 27 steps away, then turn right to begin the walk home."

Juan used mental topography retracing his uncle's words, remembering almost perfectly where the steps down and up for the curbs were, always listening intently for traffic coming from any side street. He used the walking stick awkwardly at first but then fell into a rhythm. The incessant tap, tap assuring him that he was walking in just about the center of the sidewalk. Juan couldn't believe it, but he had made it the three blocks down to the park that he and his uncle would cut through. He reached out one arm and walked at the angle he thought was the angle he and his uncle used to enter the park. He was slightly off, so it took him a few minutes to orient himself and find the large wooden sign that welcomed all into the park. It wasn't a large park by any stretch of the imagination, but to a small, blind boy making his way through it for the first time on his own it may have well been a forest.

Juan quickly found the first of the seven trees that he could ricochet off of like a pinball that would lead him almost immediately to the swings. Two sets of four swings. The third swing on the second set was broken, as one hinge had cracked over time, the wooden plank dangling helplessly toward the ground like a bird with a broken wing.

Just past the swings were the monkey bars, and to the right of them, the merry go round that Juan had actually taken a bad fall off of years ago. He had made it to the two sets of see saws and walked in between the two as he and his uncle always had. He walked about twenty steps ahead and reached out an arm and felt the metal slide that was always so hot to the touch during those long summer months.

The sound of the end of his walking stick tapping against concrete had returned and he knew he had made it to the basketball court. He found the metal chain link fence that ran the length of the court and opened up at one point to a street, his street. When he reached the corner and felt his stick tap the pole that was home to the street sign that read, Bonita Blvd, he let out a sigh of relief.

As he crossed the street, the sound of a young couple arguing in Spanish could be heard from inside the barrio taquería. He stopped for a moment, turned toward the direction of the door and inhaled. Freshly made tortillas were being thrown onto the griddle to heat, with a little butter they were a meal in and of themselves. Someone must have dropped another quarter in the jukebox, because the song by Miguel Bosé had ended a minute ago and now something slow and lovely by Ángela Carrasco y Camilo Sesto began to play, but despite the beauty of the song, the young couple argued on.

Juan turned and faced the direction of home, and carefully he crossed the street, turned right. Methodically he counted his steps feeling with his shoe the large crack in the sidewalk just in front of Mrs. Roger's house. Until finally he knew he had reached it. He stopped turned to his left and let the tapping of his walking stick guide him up the pebble path that cut through a front yard that was more dirt than grass because of the large live oak tree in the front yard that prevented the sun's light from reaching the remnants of grass below. He climbed the three steps to the concrete porch and stopped to feel the initials he had carved with a twig into the wet cement that his grandfather and uncles had poured years earlier.

He stood, folded up his cane, found the doorknob and turned it. The faint smell of bacon still lingered. He stepped through the living room bumping into an ottoman that had been left directly in the center of the room. "Who left this stupid thing here!" He heard his uncle laughing from the kitchen. Juan bit his lip and made his way into the dining room. He felt the table and found the plate that was placed in front of the chair that had been left slightly pulled out.

"Do you want me to heat up your plate mi'jo?"

"No, I'm good." Juan took a bite of cold scrambled eggs and burnt bacon. He sat there eating, thinking about everything. It's hard to say if he knew his uncle was watching him over his shoulder from time to time as he washed dishes in the kitchen. When Juan took the last bite, he pushed the plate away, the sun breaking through the curtains as he did, and ever so slowly like light entering a dark room, a smile crept across his face. Thinking back on it years later, he would count that meal as the best of his life.

About The Author

Joaquín Zihuatanejo is a poet, writer, and award-winning teacher from Dallas, Texas. He travels around the country and the world sharing an idea that is sacred to him, that idea being that everyone, especially young students should read and write poetry, as it is one of the things on this planet that connects them to their humanity. And nothing but good can come from that.

Find Joaquín online at:

Facebook: Joaquín Zihuatanejo
Twitter: @thepoetjz
Instagram: joaquinzihuatanejo
Website: www.jzthepoet.com

Joaquín has two passions in his life, his wife Aída and poetry, always in that order.

HOMEWORK: LIKE (EACH OTHER) SHARE (WITH EACH OTHER)

9 780692 235423